ASS

Life Cycles
Life Science

PROGRAM AUTHORS
Randy Bell, Ph.D.
Malcolm B. Butler, Ph.D.
Nell K. Duke, Ed.D.
Judith Lederman, Ph.D.
David W. Moore, Ph.D.
Kathy Cabe Trundle, Ph.D.

ACKNOWLEDGMENTS

Grateful acknowledgment is given to our reviewers for their time and input. Grateful acknowledgment is given to the authors, artists, photographers, museums, publishers, and agents for permission to reprint copyrighted material. Every effort has been made to secure the appropriate permission. If any omissions have been made or if corrections are required, please contact the Publisher.

Cover
(t) Digital Vision/Alamy Images, (b) Cathy Keifer/Shutterstock

Photographic Credits
7 (l) Stanislav Komogorov/iStockphoto, (r) Keith Webber Jr./iStockphoto; **8** (t) redmal/iStockphoto, (cl) Maurice van der Velden/iStockphoto, (c) Jeremy Woodhouse/PhotoDisc/Getty Images, (cr) felinda/iStockphoto, (b) Inga Spence/Visuals Unlimited; **9** Sean Locke/iStockphoto; **11** (t) George F. Mobley/National Geographic Image Collection, (b) Raymond Truelove/iStockphoto; **16** (l) YinYang/iStockphoto, (r) superdumb/Shutterstock; **17** (l) Nikolay Okhitin/Shutterstock, (c) Johnny Lye/Shutterstock, (r) Smit/Shutterstock; **19** Emilia Stasiak/Shutterstock; **22** (t) Arnold John Labrentz/Shutterstock; **22** (bl) Ladislav Susoy/Shutterstock, (bc) blewisphotography/Shutterstock, (br) Artur Tiutenko/Shutterstock.

Neither the Publisher nor the authors shall be liable for any damage that may be caused or sustained or result from conducting any of the activities in this publication without specifically following instructions, undertaking the activities without proper supervision, or failing to comply with the cautions contained herein.

Copyright © The Hampton-Brown Company, Inc., a wholly owned subsidiary of The National Geographic Society, publishing under the imprints National Geographic School Publishing and Hampton-Brown.

Teachers are authorized to reproduce the assessment materials in this Handbook in limited quantities and solely for use in their own classrooms.

Other than as authorized above, no part of this book may be reproduced or transmitted in any form or by any means, electronic or mechanical, including photocopying, recording, or by an information storage and retrieval system, without permission in writing from the Publisher.

National Geographic and the Yellow Border are registered trademarks of the National Geographic Society.

National Geographic School Publishing
Hampton-Brown
P.O. Box 223220
Carmel, California 93922

www.NGSP.com

Printed in the United States of America.

ISBN 978-0-7362-6399-3

09 10 11 12 13 14 15 16 17 10 9 8 7 6 5 4 3 2

Contents

Introduction to *National Geographic Science Life Cycles* Assessment...... 1
Program Goals 1
Assessment Design 1
Assessment Tools.. 2
Scoring Tests and Reporting Results 3

Chapter Tests 5
Chapter 1: How Do Plants Grow and Change?.................................. 7
Chapter 2: How Do Humans and Animals Grow and Change? 9
Chapter 3: How Did Some Plants and Animals Become Extinct? 11

Unit Test 13
Unit Self-Assessment 15
Unit Test: Life Cycles 16

Scoring and Reporting Tools 23
Student Profile and Answer Key: Chapter Tests 1–3 24
Student Profile and Answer Key: Unit Test 27

Inquiry Rubrics and Self-Reflections 31
Inquiry Rubrics 32
Inquiry Self-Reflections 34

Introduction

Program Goals

National Geographic Science offers research-based instruction to build scientific and content literacy for all students. The program is carefully designed to target specific state science standards while enabling students to explore the nature of science and inquiry.

Assessment Design

National Geographic Science has been designed so that frequent, varied assessment informs instruction every step of the way.

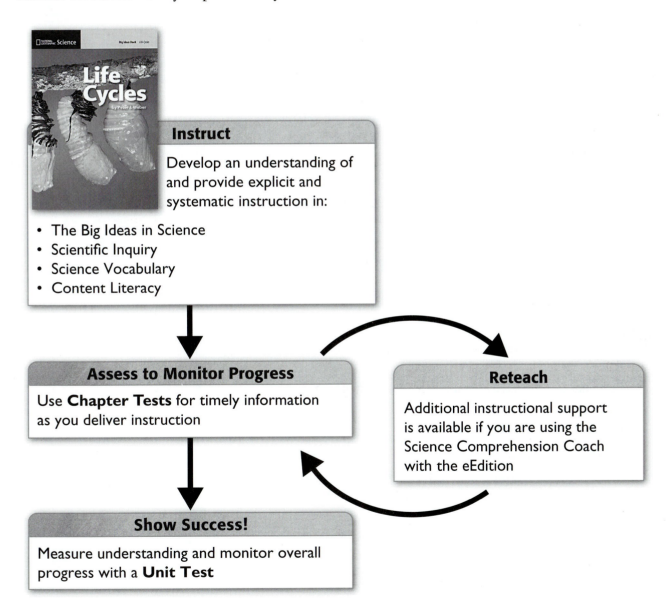

Instruct

Develop an understanding of and provide explicit and systematic instruction in:

- The Big Ideas in Science
- Scientific Inquiry
- Science Vocabulary
- Content Literacy

Assess to Monitor Progress

Use **Chapter Tests** for timely information as you deliver instruction

Reteach

Additional instructional support is available if you are using the Science Comprehension Coach with the eEdition

Show Success!

Measure understanding and monitor overall progress with a **Unit Test**

Assessment Tools

National Geographic Science offers an array of assessments in a variety of formats.

Assessment Tools	Assessment Handbook	PDFs NGSPscience.com	ExamView®
Chapter Tests • Three Chapter Tests provide immediate feedback on standards-based scientific concepts. • The tests are administered at the end of each chapter to provide an early indicator of the students' understanding and progress. • See page 5 for more information.	●	●	●
Unit Test • The Unit Test measures students' progress toward understanding the unit's Big Ideas. • The test is administered at the end of the unit to measure the students' understanding of the science standards taught in the unit. • See page 13 for more information.	●	●	●
Unit Self-Assessment • The Unit Self-Assessment empowers students to rate their own understanding of the unit concepts and share their opinions about future interests. • The self-assessment is completed by students before they take the Unit Test. • See page 13 for more information.	●	●	
Inquiry Rubrics • Inquiry Rubrics assess students' performance of skills in Inquiry activities. • The rubrics are completed after students have finished each Inquiry activity. • See page 31 for more information.	●	●	
Inquiry Self-Reflections • Inquiry Self-Reflections engage students in evaluating their own performance of inquiry skills and in sharing their opinions about the activity process. • The self-reflections are completed by students after they have finished each Inquiry activity. • See page 31 for more information.	●	●	

Scoring Tests and Reporting Results

Teachers can score tests and report results by hand. Use the Answer Keys and rubrics in the Scoring and Reporting Tools section on pages 24–28 to score the tests. Then fill out the Student and Class Profiles to report test results. See page 23 for more information.

The multiple-choice sections of the Chapter and Unit Tests can also be scored electronically. Students can take a test online through the ExamView® Test Player on a local area network, or they can mark answers on an ExamView® machine-scorable answer sheet, which is later scanned to enter data electronically. In either case, student results will be available in online reports in ExamView®.

Chapter Tests

Chapter 1: How Do Plants Grow and Change? 7
Chapter 2: How Do Humans and Animals Grow and Change? 9
Chapter 3: How Did Some Plants and Animals Become Extinct? . . . 11

Chapter Tests

Purpose and Description

A Chapter Test is available for each of the three chapters in the Life Cycles Unit. Each Chapter Test is designed to check student progress on the specific instruction within the chapter and to provide an early indicator that reteaching or additional instruction may be necessary. Chapter Tests use multiple-choice and short constructed-response items to measure the Life Science concepts taught in this unit.

Administering the Tests

Administer the test for each chapter after instruction. Allow about 10 minutes for administration. Make a copy of the test for each student.

All directions and test items, including any charts and diagrams, may be read to students. Use a copy of the test to point out directions, test items, and response areas.

Introduce the test by telling students the purpose of the test.

- To begin the test, read the directions and the first item, including the answer choices.
- Tell students how they are expected to respond to that type of item, for example, by filling in a circle.
- Give students time to work individually on the item, and allow a reasonable amount of time for them to complete it.
- Look to see that students are responding to the item in the correct manner.
- Continue to read the directions and items in the test, explaining to students how they are expected to respond to any new item formats.

Students may not use their books during the test.

Scoring the Tests and Using the Results

Score the Chapter Tests with the Answer Keys on pages 24–26. Use the Student Profiles on the same pages to determine if students need reteaching in any of the science concepts presented. For more information on scoring, see page 23.

Name _____ Date _____   **Chapter 1**

Chapter Test — How Do Plants Grow and Change?

Directions: Read each question. Then choose the correct answer.

1 How do trees start their life cycle?
- Ⓐ from bulbs
- Ⓑ from seeds
- Ⓒ from spores

2 Where are some spores found?
- Ⓐ in fruit
- Ⓑ on leaves
- Ⓒ under stems

3 At what stage does a bean plant grow beans?
- Ⓐ when it is a seed
- Ⓑ before it is a seedling
- Ⓒ after it grows flowers

4 Where are the seeds in a flowering plant?
- Ⓐ in the fruit
- Ⓑ in the leaves
- Ⓒ in the seedling

5 Look at these pictures.

young plant   parent plant

How does the young plant look like its parent?
- Ⓐ It is the same size.
- Ⓑ It has the same shape.
- Ⓒ It has the same number of branches.

6 What is true about all living things?
- Ⓐ They germinate from seeds.
- Ⓑ They grow at the same rate.
- Ⓒ They grow, change, and die.

GO ON

Name _____ Date _____ Chapter 1

Chapter Test — **How Do Plants Grow and Change?**

7 Look at this picture.

Which of these is its parent?

Ⓐ

Ⓑ

Ⓒ

8 Look at this picture of a growing pumpkin plant.

Which part is the arrow pointing to?

Ⓐ fruit

Ⓑ leaves

Ⓒ flower

Directions: Read the question. Then write your answer on the lines.

9 How is a bean seed different from a bean plant?

A bean seed _____.

A bean plant _____.

Test Score ____ /10

8

Life Cycles Assessment

Name _____ Date _____ **Chapter 2**

Chapter Test How Do Humans and Animals Grow and Change?

Directions: Read each question. Then choose the correct answer.

1. What body part helps you send messages to the rest of your body?
   - Ⓐ brain
   - Ⓑ bones
   - Ⓒ muscles

2. How does an animal's life cycle begin?
   - Ⓐ It becomes a larva.
   - Ⓑ It is born or hatched.
   - Ⓒ It grows from a seed.

3. How are reptiles different from most mammals at the start of their life cycle? Reptiles begin their lives _____.
   - Ⓐ inside eggs
   - Ⓑ as larva
   - Ⓒ in water

4. Which of these is true about the larva of a butterfly?
   - Ⓐ It flies in the air.
   - Ⓑ It eats and moves around.
   - Ⓒ It lives inside a covering.

5. Look at this picture.

   What tells you that these people are in the same family?
   - Ⓐ They are the same size.
   - Ⓑ They look the same age.
   - Ⓒ Their faces look alike.

6. In a butterfly's life cycle, which stage comes next after the egg stage?
   - Ⓐ larva
   - Ⓑ pupa
   - Ⓒ adult

7. Which of these lives in the water during the first stages of its life?
   - Ⓐ a bird
   - Ⓑ an insect
   - Ⓒ an amphibian

GO ON

Name _____ Date _____ **Chapter 2**

Chapter Test How Do Humans and Animals Grow and Change?

8 Which of these is true about all young animals?

Ⓐ They will grow to look like their parents.

Ⓑ They lose their tails when they are older.

Ⓒ They begin their life cycles in the same way.

Directions: Read the questions. Then write your answers on the lines.

9 Think about a young fish and a young dog.

How are their lives the same? _____

_____

How are their lives different? _____

_____

Test Score

_____ /10

DONE!

Life Cycles Assessment

Chapter Test: How Did Some Plants and Animals Become Extinct?

Directions: Read each question. Then choose the correct answer.

1 How do animals become extinct?

Ⓐ The adults and young all die out.

Ⓑ The adults have young that are different animals.

Ⓒ The adults change their color so they look different.

2 What can happen to animals in an area that becomes too cold?

Ⓐ The animals become extinct.

Ⓑ The animals change their life cycles.

Ⓒ The animals change how their young are born.

3 Some toads are extinct. Other toads are alive today. Why?

Ⓐ Some frog eggs hatched into toads.

Ⓑ Some toads found what they needed to survive, and others did not.

Ⓒ Toads died out, but they returned years later.

4 Look at this fossil of an extinct plant and this part of a living plant.

fossil of extinct plant

living plant

What is true about both the extinct plant and the living plant?

Ⓐ Their stems are straight.

Ⓑ Their leaves are the same shape.

Ⓒ There are many leaves coming from a stem.

Name _____ Date _____ **Chapter 3**

Chapter Test — **How Did Some Plants and Animals Become Extinct?**

5 What is one reason dinosaurs might have become extinct?

Ⓐ Their habitat was destroyed.

Ⓑ They moved somewhere else.

Ⓒ Other animals took their place.

6 How do scientists study dinosaurs?

Ⓐ They look at fossil bones they find.

Ⓑ They watch dinosaurs where they live.

Ⓒ They talk to people who observe them.

7 Which of these can make more of themselves?

Ⓐ only extinct animals

Ⓑ only living animals

Ⓒ living animals and extinct animals

8 Which of these has become extinct?

Ⓐ only dinosaurs

Ⓑ all dinosaurs and plants

Ⓒ many plants and animals

Directions: Read the sentences. Then write your answers on the lines.

9 Many animals have become extinct for different reasons. Write two reasons some animals might have or may become extinct.

1) _____

2) _____

Test Score

_____ /10

DONE!

Life Cycles Assessment

Unit Test

> Unit Self-Assessment..15
> Unit Test: Life Cycles 16

Unit Self-Assessment

Purpose and Description
The Unit Self-Assessment helps students review their own progress toward meeting specific learning objectives in the unit. Students also indicate an area of interest for further study. Make a copy of the Unit Self-Assessment for each student and have them fill it out before taking the Unit Test.

Unit Test

Purpose and Description
A Unit Test is available for the Life Cycles Unit. The Unit Test uses multiple-choice and short constructed-response items to measure student understanding of the Life Science concepts taught in this unit.

Administering the Test
Administer the Unit Test after evaluating the results of all the Chapter Tests and presenting any reteaching or additional instruction. Allow about 25 minutes for administration. Make a copy of the test for each student.

All directions and test items, including any charts and diagrams, may be read to students. Use a copy of the test to point out directions, test items, and response areas.

Introduce the test by telling students the purpose of the test.

- To begin the test, read the directions and the first item, including the answer choices.
- Tell students how they are expected to respond to that type of item, for example, by filling in a circle.
- Give students time to work individually on the item, and allow a reasonable amount of time for them to complete it.
- Look to see that students are responding to the item in the correct manner.
- Continue to read the directions and items in the test, explaining to students how they are expected to respond to any new item formats.

Students may not use their books during the test.

Unit Test

Scoring the Tests and Using the Results

Score the Unit Test with the Answer Key on page 27. Use the Student Profile on page 28 to determine if students need reteaching in any of the science concepts presented. For more information on scoring, see page 23.

Name _____ Date _____

Unit Self-Assessment — Life Cycles

Directions: Write a ✓ in the box to show the answer that is true for you.

	Yes	Not Yet
❶ I know that all living things grow, change, and die.		
❷ I know that some plants begin as seeds and then grow to look like their parents.		
❸ I know that some animals are born live and that some hatch from an egg.		
❹ I know that animals and humans grow to look like their parents.		
❺ I can tell the different human body parts.		
❻ I can talk about the stages in plant and animal life cycles.		
❼ I can talk about why some plants and animals have died out.		

Directions: Think about the things you have studied in this unit. Then finish the sentence.

❽ I am interested in learning more about _____

_____

Name _____ Date _____

Unit Test — Life Cycles

Directions: Read each question. Then choose the correct answer.

1 Where do cuttings come from?

   Ⓐ the seed

   Ⓑ the plant

   Ⓒ the fruit

2 Beans grow on a bean plant when it is _____.

   Ⓐ a seed

   Ⓑ a seedling

   Ⓒ an adult plant

3 Look at these pictures.

young plant   parent

How does the young plant look different from its parent?

   Ⓐ The young plant has a thicker stem.

   Ⓑ The young plant is smaller in size.

   Ⓒ The young plant has more leaves.

Unit Test: Life Cycles

4 Which of these shows a seed germinating?

Ⓐ

Ⓑ

Ⓒ

5 What is true about the life cycles of plants, animals, and humans?

Ⓐ They have the same number of stages.

Ⓑ They all show how living things change.

Ⓒ They all begin the same way.

6 What do flowering plants make?

Ⓐ fruit and seeds

Ⓑ fruit and spores

Ⓒ flowers and spores

7 Which stage comes before seedling?

Ⓐ fruit

Ⓑ seed

Ⓒ flower

Name _____ Date _____

Unit Test — Life Cycles

Directions: Read the sentences. Then write your answers on the lines.

8 Write one way a seedling and an older plant are alike.

_____

Write one way a seedling and an older plant are different.

_____

Directions: Read each question. Then choose the correct answer.

9 What body part helps you breathe?

Ⓐ stomach

Ⓑ heart

Ⓒ lungs

10 What body part helps you move?

Ⓐ heart

Ⓑ muscles

Ⓒ stomach

GO ON

Name _____ Date _____

Unit Test: Life Cycles

Directions: Read each question. Then choose the correct answer.

11 Look at the young mouse and its parent.

A mouse is a mammal. What is true about animals like these?

Ⓐ The young look like their parents.

Ⓑ The young are the same size as their parents.

Ⓒ The young and their parents will become more different as they grow.

12 Which of these animals hatches into a larva early in its life cycle?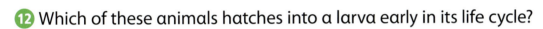

Ⓐ a fish

Ⓑ a reptile

Ⓒ an insect

13 At which stage in a frog's life cycle does it live in water?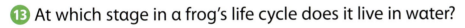

Ⓐ froglet

Ⓑ tadpole

Ⓒ adult frog

GO ON

Name _____ Date _____

Unit Test — Life Cycles

14 What is true about the life cycles of birds, insects, and amphibians?

Ⓐ They all hatch from eggs.

Ⓑ They have the same number of stages.

Ⓒ They look the same throughout their life.

15 Which of these tells you that a group of people may be part of the same family?

Ⓐ Some of their ages may be the same.

Ⓑ Some of their clothes may be the same color.

Ⓒ Some of their faces may have the same shape.

16 Which of these looks like its parent when it is first hatched?

Ⓐ frog

Ⓑ chicken

Ⓒ butterfly

Name _____ Date _____

Unit Test — Life Cycles

Directions: Read the sentence. Then write your answer on the lines.

17 Think about the stages of a chicken's life cycle. Tell what happens in two of the stages.

1) _____

_____

2) _____

_____

Directions: Read each question. Then choose the correct answer.

18 How do scientists know that the golden toad is extinct?
  Ⓐ They cannot find any more of its kind.
  Ⓑ They can find only young golden toads.
  Ⓒ They find other toads that almost look the same.

19 What is one reason a tree frog might become extinct?
  Ⓐ Too many young are born.
  Ⓑ Too much food is around.
  Ⓒ Too many trees are cut down.

GO ON

Name _____ Date _____

Unit Test — Life Cycles

20 Which of these is true about extinct plants and animals?

Ⓐ They are gone forever.

Ⓑ They all died out millions of years ago.

Ⓒ They can return after the climate is better.

21 Look at this picture of an extinct animal.

Which living animal is most like this extinct animal?

Ⓐ

Ⓑ

Ⓒ

Directions: Read the question. Then write your answer on the lines.

22 What are two ways a group of animals can become extinct?

1) _____

2) _____

Test Score ____ /25

Scoring and Reporting Tools

> Student Profile and Answer Key: Chapter Tests 1–3 24
> Student Profile and Answer Key: Unit Test 27

Student Profiles and Answer Keys

Teachers can score the students' tests and report their results by hand using the Student Profiles and Answer Keys on pages 24–28. These pages include the correct responses to multiple-choice items as well as item-specific rubrics for the short constructed-response items in each Chapter Test and the Unit Test. Make copies of each Student Profile and Answer Key for each student.

Class Profile

Use the Class Profile on page 29 to record the Chapter Test and Unit Test scores for all the students in your class.

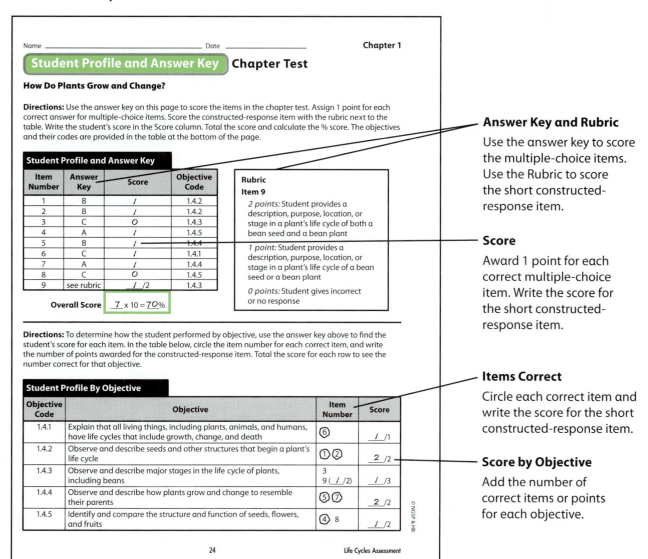

Answer Key and Rubric

Use the answer key to score the multiple-choice items. Use the Rubric to score the short constructed-response item.

Score

Award 1 point for each correct multiple-choice item. Write the score for the short constructed-response item.

Items Correct

Circle each correct item and write the score for the short constructed-response item.

Score by Objective

Add the number of correct items or points for each objective.

Name _____ Date _____ **Chapter 1**

Student Profile and Answer Key | Chapter Test

How Do Plants Grow and Change?

Directions: Use the answer key on this page to score the items in the chapter test. Assign 1 point for each correct answer for multiple-choice items. Score the constructed-response item with the rubric next to the table. Write the student's score in the Score column. Total the score and calculate the % score. The objectives and their codes are provided in the table at the bottom of the page.

Student Profile and Answer Key

Item Number	Answer Key	Score	Objective Code
1	B		1.4.2
2	B		1.4.2
3	C		1.4.3
4	A		1.4.5
5	B		1.4.4
6	C		1.4.1
7	A		1.4.4
8	C		1.4.5
9	see rubric	___/2	1.4.3
Overall Score		___ x 10 = ___%	

Rubric

Item 9

2 points: Student provides a description, purpose, location, or stage in a plant's life cycle of both a bean seed and a bean plant

1 point: Student provides a description, purpose, location, or stage in a plant's life cycle of a bean seed or a bean plant

0 points: Student gives incorrect or no response

Directions: To determine how the student performed by objective, use the answer key above to find the student's score for each item. In the table below, circle the item number for each correct item, and write the number of points awarded for the constructed-response item. Total the score for each row to see the number correct for that objective.

Student Profile By Objective

Objective Code	Objective	Item Number	Score
1.4.1	Explain that all living things, including plants, animals, and humans, have life cycles that include growth, change, and death	6	___/1
1.4.2	Observe and describe seeds and other structures that begin a plant's life cycle	1 2	___/2
1.4.3	Observe and describe major stages in the life cycle of plants, including beans	3 9 (___/2)	___/3
1.4.4	Observe and describe how plants grow and change to resemble their parents	5 7	___/2
1.4.5	Identify and compare the structure and function of seeds, flowers, and fruits	4 8	___/2

Life Cycles Assessment

© NGSP & HB

Name _____ Date _____ Chapter 2

Student Profile and Answer Key — Chapter Test

How Do Humans and Animals Grow and Change?

Directions: Use the answer key on this page to score the items in the chapter test. Assign 1 point for each correct answer for multiple-choice items. Score the constructed-response item with the rubric next to the table. Write the student's score in the Score column. Total the score and calculate the % score. The objectives and their codes are provided in the table at the bottom of the page.

Student Profile and Answer Key

Item Number	Answer Key	Score	Objective Code
1	A		1.4.8
2	B		1.4.6
3	A		1.4.9
4	B		1.4.6
5	C		1.4.7
6	A		1.4.11
7	C		1.4.9
8	A		1.4.10
9	see rubric	___/2	1.4.9
Overall Score		___ x 10 = ___%	

Rubric

Item 9

2 points: Student indicates a similarity and a difference, including their life cycles stages, their habitat, similarities to their parents, or how they grow

1 point: Student indicates a similarity or a difference

0 points: Student gives incorrect or no response

Directions: To determine how the student performed by objective, use the answer key above to find the student's score for each item. In the table below, circle the item number for each correct item, and write the number of points awarded for the constructed-response item. Total the score for each row to see the number correct for that objective.

Student Profile By Objective

Objective Code	Objective	Item Number	Score
1.4.6	Observe and describe major stages in the life cycle of animals	2 4	___/2
1.4.7	Recognize and identify ways that humans resemble their parents	5	___/1
1.4.8	Distinguish human body parts (brain, heart, lungs, stomach, muscles, and skeleton)	1	___/1
1.4.9	Identify and compare the early stages in the life cycles of animals	3 7 9 (___/2)	___/4
1.4.10	Recognize that animals resemble their parents	8	___/1
1.4.11	Identify and sequence the stages of an animal's life cycle	6	___/1

Name _____ Date _____

Chapter 3

Student Profile and Answer Key — Chapter Test

How Did Some Plants and Animals Become Extinct?

Directions: Use the answer key on this page to score the items in the chapter test. Assign 1 point for each correct answer for multiple-choice items. Score the constructed-response item with the rubric next to the table. Write the student's score in the Score column. Total the score and calculate the % score. The objectives and their codes are provided in the table at the bottom of the page.

Student Profile and Answer Key

Item Number	Answer Key	Score	Objective Code
1	A		1.4.12
2	A		1.4.12
3	B		1.4.13
4	C		1.4.13
5	A		1.4.12
6	A		1.4.12
7	B		1.4.13
8	C		1.4.12
9	see rubric	____/2	1.4.12
Overall Score		____ x 10 = ____%	

Rubric

Item 9

2 points: Student writes two causes of extinction

1 point: Student writes one cause of extinction

0 points: Student gives incorrect or no response

Directions: To determine how the student performed by objective, use the answer key above to find the student's score for each item. In the table below, circle the item number for each correct item, and write the number of points awarded for the constructed-response item. Total the score for each row to see the number correct for that objective.

Student Profile By Objective

Objective Code	Objective	Item Number	Score
1.4.12	Recognize that some kinds of organisms that once lived on Earth have completely disappeared	1 2 5 6 8 9 (____/2)	____/7
1.4.13	Compare extinct life forms with living organisms	3 4 7	____/3

Name _____ Date _____   **Life Cycles**

Student Profile and Answer Key — Unit Test

Directions: Use the answer key on this page to score the items in the unit test. Assign 1 point for each correct answer for multiple-choice items. Score the constructed-response items with the rubrics on this page. Write the student's score in the Score column. Total the score and calculate the % score. The objectives and their codes are provided in a table on the next page.

Student Profile and Answer Key

Item Number	Answer Key	Score	Objective Code
1	B		1.4.2
2	C		1.4.3
3	B		1.4.4
4	A		1.4.3
5	B		1.4.1
6	A		1.4.5
7	B		1.4.3
8	see rubric	___/2	1.4.4
9	C		1.4.8
10	B		1.4.8
11	A		1.4.10
12	C		1.4.9
13	B		1.4.11
14	A		1.4.6
15	C		1.4.7
16	B		1.4.10
17	see rubric	___/2	1.4.6
18	A		1.4.12
19	C		1.4.12
20	A		1.4.12
21	B		1.4.13
22	see rubric	___/2	1.4.12

Overall Score   ___ x 4 = ___ %

Rubrics

Item 8

2 points: Student provides one way that a seedling and an older plant are alike and one way that they are different

1 point: Student provides one way that a seedling and an older plant are alike or one way that they are different

0 points: Student gives incorrect or no response

Item 17

2 points: Student describes two stages of a chicken's life cycle (egg, chick, adult)

1 point: Student describes one stage of a chicken's life cycle

0 points: Student gives incorrect or no response

Item 22

2 points: Student provides two ways a group of animals can become extinct, including climate change, destruction of habitat, animals not meeting their needs, or animals not reproducing

1 point: Student provides one way a group of animals can become extinct

0 points: Student gives incorrect or no response

Name _____ Date _____ **Life Cycles**

Student Profile and Answer Key — Unit Test continued

Directions: To determine how the student performed by objective, use the answer key on the previous page to find the student's score for each item. In the table below, circle the item number for each correct item, and write the number of points awarded for the constructed-response item. Total the score for each row to see the number correct for that objective.

Student Profile By Objective

Objective Code	Objective	Item Number	Score
1.4.1	Explain that all living things, including plants, animals, and humans, have life cycles that include growth, change, and death	5	____/1
1.4.2	Observe and describe seeds and other structures that begin a plant's life cycle	1	____/1
1.4.3	Observe and describe major stages in the life cycle of plants, including beans	2 4 7	____/3
1.4.4	Observe and describe how plants grow and change to resemble their parents	3 8 (____/2)	____/3
1.4.5	Identify and compare the structure and function of seeds, flowers, and fruits	6	____/1
1.4.6	Observe and describe major stages in the life cycle of animals	14 17 (____/2)	____/3
1.4.7	Recognize and identify ways that humans resemble their parents	15	____/1
1.4.8	Distinguish human body parts (brain, heart, lungs, stomach, muscles, and skeleton)	9 10	____/2
1.4.9	Identify and compare the early stages in the life cycles of animals	12	____/1
1.4.10	Recognize that animals resemble their parents	11 16	____/2
1.4.11	Identify and sequence the stages of an animal's life cycle	13	____/1
1.4.12	Recognize that some kinds of organisms that once lived on Earth have completely disappeared	18 19 20 22 (____/2)	____/5
1.4.13	Compare extinct life forms with living organisms	21	____/1

Class Profile | Life Cycles

Directions: Write student names below. Record student Chapter Test and Unit Test scores in the columns to the right.

Student Name	Chapter Test 1	Chapter Test 2	Chapter Test 3	Unit Test

Inquiry Rubrics and Self-Reflections

> Inquiry Rubrics 32
> Inquiry Self-Reflections 34

Inquiry Rubrics

Purpose and Description

Inquiry Rubrics are provided for scoring each of the four Inquiry activities from the Science Inquiry Book of the Life Cycles Unit. Each Inquiry Rubric is specific to the activity and lists the skills that students will demonstrate in that activity.

Make a copy of the rubric pages for each student. Evaluate each student after completing an activity. Assign 1 to 4 points for the student's performance on each of the skills, and then assign an overall score. Record the scores on each student's copy of the rubric.

Inquiry Self-Reflections

Purpose and Description

The Inquiry Self-Reflection, written in student-friendly, accessible language, helps students evaluate what they have learned by doing each activity. It allows students to review their own progress toward meeting specific skill goals. Students indicate their progress in attaining activity-specific skills. In addition, students are asked how well their group worked together, what went well or could be improved, and/or what was most memorable.

Make a copy of each Inquiry Self-Reflection for each student. After finishing each activity, ask students to complete the form. You may read the Inquiry Self-Reflection statements and questions aloud to the class.

Name _____

Inquiry Rubrics — Life Cycles

Explore Activity

Date _____

Directions: Use the scale descriptions next to the table to guide your assessment of the student's work. Assess each item separately, and then decide on one overall score. Circle the score for each item and the overall score.

Inquiry Rubric	Scale			
The student **observed** the bean seed and seedling.	4	3	2	1
The student **recorded** the observations.	4	3	2	1
The student sequenced illustrations representing different stages of a bean plant's life cycle.	4	3	2	1
The student **compared** observations with others.	4	3	2	1
The student **shared** observations and **conclusions** with other students.	4	3	2	1
Overall Score	4	3	2	1

Scale Descriptions

4: Student performs the skill with **thorough** understanding.
3: Student performs the skill with **adequate** understanding.
2: Student performs the skill with **basic** understanding.
1: Student performs the skill with **limited** understanding.

Directed Inquiry

Date _____

Directions: Use the scale descriptions next to the table to guide your assessment of the student's work. Assess each item separately, and then decide on one overall score. Circle the score for each item and the overall score.

Inquiry Rubric	Scale			
The student **observed** the stages of the life cycle of a butterfly using a hand lens.	4	3	2	1
The student recorded his or her observations.	4	3	2	1
The student **compared** his or her observations with others.	4	3	2	1
The student compared the stages of the butterfly life cycle.	4	3	2	1
The student **shared** observations and **conclusions** with other students.	4	3	2	1
Overall Score	4	3	2	1

Scale Descriptions

4: Student performs the skill with **thorough** understanding.
3: Student performs the skill with **adequate** understanding.
2: Student performs the skill with **basic** understanding.
1: Student performs the skill with **limited** understanding.

Name _____

Inquiry Rubrics Life Cycles

Guided Inquiry

Date _____

Directions: Use the scale descriptions next to the table to guide your assessment of the student's work. Assess each item separately, and then decide on one overall score. Circle the score for each item and the overall score.

Inquiry Rubric	Scale			
The student **observed** a shell and recorded the observations.	4	3	2	1
The student made a **model** fossil of a shell.	4	3	2	1
The student **compared** his or her observations with others.	4	3	2	1
The students compared his or her model fossil to a picture of a fossil of an extinct organism.	4	3	2	1
The student **shared** results and **conclusions** with others.	4	3	2	1
Overall Score	4	3	2	1

Scale Descriptions

4: Student performs the skill with **thorough** understanding.

3: Student performs the skill with **adequate** understanding.

2: Student performs the skill with **basic** understanding.

1: Student performs the skill with **limited** understanding.

Open Inquiry

Date _____

Directions: Use the scale descriptions next to the table to guide your assessment of the student's work. Assess each item separately, and then decide on one overall score. Circle the score for each item and the overall score.

Inquiry Rubric	Scale			
The student generated or chose a **question** to investigate.	4	3	2	1
The student planned an **investigation**.	4	3	2	1
The student made and compared **observations** and collected and recorded **data**.	4	3	2	1
The student formed a **conclusion** and explained results based on evidence from the collected data and observations.	4	3	2	1
The student **shared** observations and conclusions with other students.	4	3	2	1
Overall Score	4	3	2	1

Scale Descriptions

4: Student performs the skill with **thorough** understanding.

3: Student performs the skill with **adequate** understanding.

2: Student performs the skill with **basic** understanding.

1: Student performs the skill with **limited** understanding.

Name _____

Explore Activity Self-Reflection — Life Cycles

Directions: Write a ✓ in the box to show the answer that is true for you.

	Yes	Not Yet
❶ I can observe bean seeds and seedlings.		
❷ I can record my observations.		
❸ I can put pictures in order to show a bean plant's life cycle.		
❹ I can compare observations with others.		
❺ I can share observations and conclusions with others.		

Directions: Write an answer to each question.

❻ What could you improve about this inquiry? _____

_____

_____

_____

❼ What will you remember most from this inquiry? _____

_____

_____

_____

Name _____

Directed Inquiry Self-Reflection — Life Cycles

Directions: Write a ✓ in the box to show the answer that is true for you.

	Yes	Not Yet
❶ I can observe the stages of the life cycle of a butterfly with a hand lens.		
❷ I can record my observations.		
❸ I can compare my observations with others.		
❹ I can compare the stages of the butterfly life cycle.		
❺ I can share observations and conclusions with others.		

Directions: Write an answer to each question.

❻ How well did your group work together? _____

_____

_____

_____

❼ What will you remember most from this inquiry? _____

_____

_____

_____

Name _____

Guided Inquiry Self-Reflection — Life Cycles

Directions: Write a ✓ in the box to show the answer that is true for you.

	Yes	Not Yet
❶ I can observe a shell and record my observations.		
❷ I can make a model fossil of a shell.		
❸ I can compare my observations with others.		
❹ I can compare my model fossil to a picture of a fossil of an extinct animal.		
❺ I can share results and conclusions with others.		

Directions: Write an answer to each question.

❻ What could you improve about this inquiry? _____
_____
_____
_____

❼ What could you do to help your group work together better? _____
_____
_____
_____

Name _____

Open Inquiry Self-Reflection — Life Cycles

Directions: Write a ✓ in the box to show the answer that is true for you.

	Yes	Not Yet
❶ I can make up or choose a question to investigate.		
❷ I can plan an investigation.		
❸ I can make and compare observations and collect and record data.		
❹ I can form a conclusion and explain results based on data and observations.		
❺ I can share observations and conclusions with others.		

Directions: Write an answer to each question.

❻ What did you do well? _____

_____

_____

_____

❼ What will you remember to do in your next inquiry? _____

_____

_____

_____